CW00524583

Foreword

I was a mess. I was only fifty years old and I had deteriorating joints and bones. I was in the process of waiting many months for a knee replacement. I could barely walk and not drive. Even before that, I had spent a decade trying to manage the symptoms of painful rheumatoid arthritis amongst other things. My worst nightmare had come true. I was housebound, limited and nowhere to go except surrender to the realisation that the answer to all my problems was me. I was the centre of my nightmare but I came to understand that I am also the centre of my best dream!

As my entire life revolved around me, I reacted to it willingly (albeit unconsciously) and my reactions set off even more of the same or similar experiences. I did not realise then that *how* I reacted, thought, created and behaved carved out my reality. Like a sculptor chipping away at a large, beautiful piece of marble, every chip made a difference. I needed to see that I had to slow down my thinking and chip away with much greater care, confidence, skill, love, intuition and with all my being. I must add that it was not my 'fault' and I was not to 'blame'. Blame and shame are simply unhelpful thoughts at any stage of life and about anything. If I knew better, I would have had different thoughts and made different choices. I still may have experienced some illness but with better care, support and professional help, I may have recovered much more quickly. For example, a deep belief of worthlessness can potentially lead to not being proactive, not standing up for yourself and not making progress in life.

It's in the *how* that creates our personality. We do create personality, after all we are not set in stone! Every personality will respond differently to life's challenges and circumstances in how and what they do. For example, *how* do you respond to life? With love, compassion, gratitude? Excitement, joy, anticipation? Caution, procrastination, apathy? Trepidation, avoidance, fear? Resentment, anger, bitterness? Sometimes, it's not even a conscious process or decision until you wake up. Until life gets too messy, too painful and too impossible to live anymore that it jolts you awake to shine a light on who you're being, how you're responding and what you truly want in life. And then, the journey really begins because it's then you take back the reins. You realise you had the power all along and that you are at the centre of it all. So, don't be hard on yourself for falling into a nightmare or a life less than you want. See it this way, the hardships woke you up, the challenges made you stronger, the nightmares gave you courage and now, *now* you are ready for your best dreams to come true.

Introduction

The poems in this book came to me usually after meditation or moments of inspiration. Please bear in mind that the hardships in my life were mostly the driving force that guided me into meditation, writing poetry and reading up on the subject of expanding consciousness. Therefore, the hardships were the catalysts and the triggers that built the momentum and directed me onto a better path. So often I would be disheartened by my health issues, life's struggles and feelings of helplessness. Even though I was writing uplifting poetry, meditating and learning more, I still seemed to experience the same hardships. Then, I reached rock bottom, absolute rock bottom. I completely surrendered. I thought I'd reached that place many times prior but you know when you've really hit rock bottom because you know with **ALL** your being you cannot live your life like that anymore. You must change. You must and **WANT** to change to live a new and better life. It's like the hardships and gate posts were saying No! Not this way! There's another path for you and a better path. And you can take all that pride, frustration, hurt and sorrow to turn you around and **PROPEL** you onto that better path like rocket fuel. These poems were also signs albeit less 'shouty' signs. It's as if they've been saying all along, this way, come this way. That's the thing about messages and signs from the heart and soul, they tend to be much more gentle albeit relentless.

So, why do we ignore the signs?!

Everyone is different and their reasons are unique. However, we're born into a society that has its beliefs and systems already set up and integrated. We adopt or take on these beliefs and systems unconsciously until we want to rebel against some of them. At some point, we start questioning, are they really supporting me, my family and my community? The questioning is a very powerful place to be but the next step in *how* we respond is crucial. Sure, we can fight them, complain, campaign against them, oppose them, and sometimes that works. But what if we end up creating more of the same? What if the rocket fuel of all that frustrated energy is instead used to create new beliefs and systems? This applies to us as individuals as well as communities. What if we look for and listen to the signs that are guiding us onto better paths?

Everything is energy. At a quantum physics level or higher spiritual level nothing is good or bad. It. just. Is. So, a fresh approach could be to take all that energy built up for fighting, rebelling, resisting and direct it into what we *do* want. Do we want deeper connection, more abundance, safety and shelter for all so everyone's needs are met? Do we want more creative opportunities, more shared visions, greater clarity, more acceptance and love? Do we want more collaboration, combined skills, inventions and unity? Plus so much more! When we're clear about what we *do* want, we can see the signs much more clearly that guide us that way. Listening to our intuition is a big part of understanding what we truly want. Fortunately, there are so many methods to help us listen. From meditation, nature walks, prayer, exercise, sports, hobbies, poetry, writing, singing, crafting to painting and much more! I do believe the listening gets easier when you let yourself decide what you *don't* want. It's like clearing out a cupboard. For example, if I don't want all this, then what *do* I want? Ahhhhh, now I'm back on focus and the signs will come!

If you're reading this book, then please accept it as a sign!

I do feel the need to repeat that if you've found yourself on a path less than desirable, you must not berate yourself or be hard. After all, our life doesn't come with a manual! We learn and grow, and adapt. We remember, when we surrender to it, that we have an innate, inner, central guiding system. And even then, chances are we're out of practice listening to it and it takes time.

I totally understand if you're in a dark place and how challenging that is, I've been there more times than I can count. Sometimes just having enough hope gets you through.Then, soon you feel able to open up to new thoughts and receive new things. A poem that has been a great comfort and reminder to me is, '**I'm actually really lucky**' at the end of the book. It reminds me that I have my foundations already in place. I have all my senses (albeit I'm deaf in one ear), I have love and compassion, I can be creative, I can see beauty around me, I've learned to slow down to enjoy more and my inner child is alive and well. These foundations are priceless.These foundations are the core of building a good life, a great life. Your foundations may be slightly or somewhat different but you have them. Just like the basis of a good book, you have the tools and means available to create a story and a life that is magical.

We all need help in life sometimes with inspiration and impetus. If you're in need of some direction and a reminder of how powerful you are in creating your reality, let this book and its poems steer you onto a better path. Every poem in this book has been written with the intention of raising vibration, uplifting mood and creating a wonderful life full of joy, abundance, love and peace.

I hope that you enjoy reading these poems and also deeply feel the essence and power of them. May this book ignite your spark, help you realise your own best dreams and live a life better than you could ever have imagined!

Calling all the dreamers!

That dream you have that's always here
But seems to take so long to appear
Is waiting for YOU to begin
To stop and go 'real' deep within

So, stop right now for goodness sake
And all your worries now forsake
Focus then on all your senses
Give up the lies and pretences

Ask yourself what ignites your soul
And what are the best of your goals
Look at the details and small things
For these are where your true heart sings

The smells, the fragrance and the air
Lifting you higher without a care
The taste, the flavours and the food
Erupting taste buds and your mood

The movement, the dance and the flow
In harmony everywhere you go
The sights, the visions and the view
With more excitement coming through

The touch, the feel and the caress
Evaporating any stress
The sound, the music and the tone
Always held and never alone

Embody your dream and then smile
It really need not take a while
As you're the master of your dream
Creating an awesome live stream!

The world needs to see your passion

The world needs to see your passion
Your true colours and your true being
All your ideas, your deepest desires
And everything that you are 'seeing'

Your passion lights up the world
Because you're on fire, burning bright
It's you without fears, without limits
It's you with a clear, sharp sense of sight

The world needs to see your passion
Own your passion, set it free
It touches everyone in this world
So, be it, see it, own it, let it be.

Together we create a rainbow.

Sunrise

When the light rises on this new day
I relish the words it has to say
That all things will eventually pass
They will spin by supremely fast
So soak up all the moments you love
And I'll keep shining from here above
Bask in the fragrance you love awhile
Breathe it in longer until you smile
Wallow in tastes that spring back your joy
Create with nature - life's greatest toy
Feel deeply with your sensitive hands
Explore many different kinds of lands
Swim in the beauty of varied views
Celebrate freedom of thoughts you choose
Listen to the songs that lift you high
Raising spirits with no need to try.

Steeped in my heart

I'm steeped and held so deep in my heart
The drama above that's off the chart
Will remain detached while I bathe here
And stormy clouds will soon become cleared

My heart knows best and envelopes me
She's the love and the epitome
Guiding me to relax and breathe deep
So, I let myself soak more and steep.

I am Here. HEAR I am

No more torn apart and expectantly waiting
Hiding from the anger and worse still placating
No, I've remembered this truth once again to tell
That I am Here, HEAR I am, and I am so well

Frustration is born from the ways of not seeing
For all along it's my perspective that's freeing
The most vast, loving and extraordinary me
Is here, HEAR I am, ready and able to be

My true sound rings expansive and fills my world up
If I let it, miracles spring free from this cup
I am here, HEAR I am, I am listening so well
And I am ready for this new chapter to tell.

The Lake of Endless Possibilities

I forgive all to be here
To swim in this lake so clear
Blame and shame have long since gone
I'm letting love be the one.

I am so much more

Look at me now and look well
See the scars my stories tell
See the soft and wrinkled skin
Sometimes crying deep within

See my mistakes in large mounds
And hear my forgiving sounds
See the mask that's wearing thin
Listen to the voice that wins

All of it is me and more
Kept in my memory store
But to regret I must not
As the truth I had forgot

That I am so much more
Not just what went before
Here I stand all new and proud
Singing this song f**king loud!

You are part of a much grander reveal

I am a woman - my hormones are racing
I'm 50 - illusions of ageing I'm facing
I feel like a mess and perhaps I have been
And too damn worried about how I am seen

Not special or grand, or changing the world
My hopes and dreams long since unfurled
Into the wind they've gone, and blown far from me
Barely can I remember them clearly

Yet, perhaps I forgot or didn't then see
That just being a woman here is crazy
And for that reason alone I must praise
All women who this 'game of life' do raise

The courage and strength to live, grow and expand
In a world where growth feels like walking through sand
I salute you women for your persistence
When the patriarchy squash your existence

But when a goddess clears the sand from her eyes
And sees clearly all the illusions and lies
A new world view reveals itself and awakes
War, poverty, and injustice it forsakes

Women, know that no matter how small you feel
You are all part of a much grander reveal
So then, wash your eyes and clear away the sand
And in your power, love and peace proudly stand!

What love feels like

I return to this place - a cocoon retreat
Held in warmth and comfort that cannot be leaked
Here, there's no pressure only time to just be
Vast open space to breathe deeply and rest free

No judgements or scorn can ever creep in here
As the air, flow and consciousness is so clear
And when I do hear voices they only say
Kind things that lift my spirits such a long way

There is patience, listening and I'm fully heard
No miscommunication that's so absurd
Just held with the greatest respect and deep care
A great love that's within me and everywhere.

A blank canvas of endless possibilities

Here I am, held in this moment of no judgement
A blank canvas of endless possibilities
A space full of compassion, stillness and love
As I draw in the light and wisdom from above

No expectation and no rush or demands
Only patience, peace and being held so warm
Allowing me to take my time in all of this
To create a story that aligns with my bliss

The inside out tortoise

I was born with my shell deep inside
It protects me and much more aside
If I'm feeling overwhelmed or pain
I retreat then to my shell again
For inside my shell is perfect peace
And also where all wanting does cease
Here, I feel all the comfort and care
No needing or desire to compare
I feel praised, held, nurtured and at ease
No requirements to fit in and please
In fact, in here is the perfect chord
Perfect balance that I can afford
And so, when I emerge from my shell
I bring with me this story to tell.

A whole new path has been laid

I'm holding out my hand to you
Please take it now without delay
It's alright, no need to be afraid
A whole new path has been laid

This path that we have built for you
A space of glorious beauty and wonder
So filled with warmth, comfort and love
Yes, just like our heaven above

We felt the pain and we burdened the sorrows
But it had to be this way, you see
To pave the way for you my dears
So you felt safe to release your fears

Come, join us now in this beautiful realm
It's here, right now, awaiting your presence
It's not a dream, or a distant place
But the most loving and heavenly, sacred space.

Energy

My energy here is all my own
But myself I wanted to disown
Only because all the traumas past
Made me think suffering would last

Yet, here I am looking deep within
Remembering that I am sovereign
I have power for I am THE WAY
It's not beyond me or gone astray

I can adjust my frequency more
When I recall there's plenty in store
My roots are deep and connected now
So, peace, love and joy, I do allow.

My movie reel

For every delicious feeling I have
And every rich experience I feel
I know that I am creating much more
Of moments like this in my movie reel

Either in the bath with warm water bliss
Eating fruit smoothies with taste buds alive
Or stood by the river that's clear and fresh
I know that I can reignite and thrive

Letting myself dwell in these rich moments
Is the greatest investment I could make
Allowing my senses to open up
So that I'm fully present and awake

I'm no longer out of sync or control
Instead, I'm the director of my realm
I choose how my days and life will unfold
I am grounded and relaxed at my helm.

Dwelling in wonder

When a child's eyes like discs open up wide
And a smile upon their face does glide
So too their precious lungs swell with air
As they see in wonder without care

Knowledge is such a very great thing
And the wisdom of life lessons they bring
Yet, the moments our heart's really soar
Are when we glow with wonder once more.

This now precious moment

This now precious moment is my everything
Here, I experience what my choices bring
I welcome harmonies that lift my spirits
I tune into songs with refreshing lyrics

I feel my heart and surrender to her lead
Because with her guidance I am always freed
I do not invite or welcome those beings
That cannot tune into what my heart's seeing

I listen well to my heart's rhythmic hum
For my heart is my power and protective drum
She's my cello, my instrument and my muse
On her vast ocean I joyfully cruise

If emotions arise like guilt, blame or shame
I turn my vision to a much wider frame
And I keep on looking through that window pane
Where forgiving love is the essence that reigns

Vast oceans, lakes, mountains untouched and so wild
Like the pure laughter of an innocent child
Become my focus in this now moment bliss
This precious *now* moment where nothing's amiss.

Only love reminds us we're completely whole

What greater act of courage than to shine a light
On all that prevents us from loving and true sight
To see all those places abandoned and so cold
Where only love reminds us we're completely whole.

You are

You are all the stars, the moon and the sun
Plus all the magic since time had begun.

Look up to the stars

With my feet firmly on the ground
I breathe in earth's beautiful sound
And as I look up to the sky
I feel my spirit soaring high

In the starlit sky, I immerse
Dwelling in this vast universe
And by my heart that sings so loud
I break through any lasting shroud

The light in me now does reign
My love and power so free again
I only had to listen well
For this divine story to tell.

The fire in me

See the fire swell up in me
A force of good and clarity
Too long I tired to dampen it
For fear it was too brightly lit

But fires were meant for burning
To help us be more discerning
A driver if you will, for life
Burning through discontent that's rife

I'll no more suppress this fire
But let it help me rise higher
And with my heart it will reign
In sovereign union once again!

Dear universe,

Within my heart is a well
With many stories to tell
And it's full of options vast
So my rod of dreams, I cast

I keep my mind open wide
Plus with my spirit confide
To ensure my bait is bright
And my best dreams see the light

But if my rod makes a catch
That to my dreams are not matched
I gently let that catch go
And return to what I know

I let my love be my guide
And aim to enjoy the ride
Love will always set me right
Along with my inner sight

So again, I'll make a cast
Leave behind all those things past
Breathing in the magic now
For my best dreams I allow.

The window of NOW

In this present moment I saw some curtains so clear
They opened to make visible a window appear
A soft voice whispered, 'That window is your everything'
It is the place where your heart and mind together sing

It's the NOW place where dreams and life happen just for you
Whereas the curtains are your past life and future too
Instead, draw back those curtains and gently focus your gaze
On the window of NOW and be ready to be amazed

The window gets bigger and bigger, the more you see
And from your past life and your future, you'll be free
With freedom, you open to vast possibilities
To parts of you with greater scope and abilities

This window wants to help you expand your mind and heart
It has plenty of wisdom and knowledge to impart
Just simply draw back the curtains when you are ready
Take your time, be patient, loving, gentle and steady.

Making space to breathe

Declaring some space as mine
To breathe deep and take my time
Is strength and rich endeavour
That serves me well forever

Great is this new boundary
A rich and golden foundry
Created by my making
Dis-ease it'll be forsaking

Peace and love do reign in here
With love now flowing more clear
In this space I've opened up
For new life to fill my cup.

The heroine's journey

Fear wanted to write her story and her life

Fear would approach often with lines full of strife

But then, she learned to turn and to face her fear

And into the shadows it would disappear

This fear did not want responsibility

Or to do anything intentionally

Fear itself was afraid and of light so scared

Because it felt less than worthy and impaired

Before long, the heroine realised this

And decided her own journey was amiss

The only way was to step forward again

Into her very own light to let love reign

She knew this required great focus and play

To make her story go a much better way

The spotlight became a friend this time around

As she chose to sing in tune with love's own sound.

Love's own sound rang of joy, compassion and peace

Replenishing every part and every piece

That once had faded into those shrunken rooms

Now sprung back to life with magnificent blooms!

Who are you?

Who are you when you smile
Breathing deeply all the while
Eyes wide open, seeing
Body fluid, freeing
Mind alert, in wonder
Heart beating, like thunder
Like nature unfolding
So vast and amazing?
Can you remember now
And the REAL you, allow?

Compassion

Compassion, I can see
Will be the new currency
Creating a whole new realm
Of which we're at the helm

Yes, this ship we navigate
Is much more than random fate
But only in the silence we can hear
How to once again learn to steer

There's no need to remain in port
With so much love and infinite support
Beyond the walls of separation
Are the feelings of total elation

Sink into the silent space
And you'll remember from this place
Can be born a whole new way of being
One that is loving and totally freeing.

Dripping with kindness

In this dimension, where I am now
Is dripping with kindness, that I allow
It's saturated with love everywhere
Filled to the brim with support, warmth and care

This knowing invites me to soak it up
To let this resonance fill up my cup
You see, hardship is impossible here
Where the water of knowing's crystal clear

No disease, tension or woes can remain
So drenched with love is this vast open plane
Never separate or far but always here
It's within and without, so crystal clear.

It's in your breath

If you want to know who you are
It's in your breath, so near not far
All your dreams, your heart's desire
It's in your breath, your burning fire

End the searching, the seeking beyond
It's in your breath, your magical wand
Let it unfold, your natural state
It's in your breath, inevitable fate

Even in dreaming your greatest dream
It's in your breath, an effortless stream
All of this truth is waiting for you
It's in your breath, let go, be true.

All That Is and Divine Expression

When I can say these words without a flinch
That I'm 'All That Is and Divine Expression'
I know that I have transcended ego
And learned that difficult and painful lesson

Now I see clearly a path before me
To create in a most deliberate way
That serves me better and all of the world
A way that is driven by conscious pray.

Dance in harmony and joy - you might as well

Seeing as all your cells vibrate anyway
It seems to me they might as well vibrate
In a way that feels good and really uplifting
Imagine their dance and everything shifting

See them go about their merry way
Even during challenges and other issues
Skipping, dancing and warm-hearted smiles
They dance their way through all the trials

If you were to see your cells through a telescope
You'd know what I mean by this merry dance
But every dance has a different story to tell
So, dance in harmony and joy - you might as well.

Thoughts of overwhelm

Thoughts of overwhelm can take over me
Telling me in life there's no guarantee
Uncertainty relentless, burning through
But I know there's another clearer view

And from that view I choose to see the prize
Which for me is to see with loving eyes
When I focus on what I love so dear
My life falls gently into peace more clear

Maybe my focus got blurred and faded
By events that left me feeling jaded
Yet now, I have a choice all of my own
A power to choose from my loving throne.

I am HOME

I am HOME when in my heart I listen well
Engulfed in her enormous loving swell
Even if listening goes against the grain
I'll be living my best life beyond the pain.

fEAR is guiding me back to peace

Perhaps then, fEAR is a chance to hEAR
To listen well and to get more clEAR

So, I listen to this fearful stuff
Soon, I come to realise enough

That a lot of fearful thoughts are lies
And I don't need to be to them tied

The stuff I can't control I release
Then, I sit back into greater peace

This moment now is all that exists
Where in my surrender peace persists.

True love

True love is not in high towers
True love has much greater power
True love lies in the weakest breath
True love does not know end or death

True love will not demand or judge
True love knows not of the hard trudge
True love whispers that all's alright
True love gives us much clearer sight

True love will gently navigate
Lead us into more peaceful states
Where we can rest and breathe so well
And stories of love we can tell.

Good fortune is pre-sent

A loving wave will always reclaim
Healing love and cleansing shame
Upon our shores it ebbs and flows
Across the cosmos it sure grows

Yes it's possible, yes it's a dream
It's here right now as far as I can glean
The pleasure and ecstasy is for one and all
And even more members are hearing this call

Good fortune and joy unfolds in this way
And every member is invited to pray
That this good fortune is now pre-sent
And all we need is to give our consent.

Utterly freed

Accessing the eternal at any time

Such blissful timelessness is just sublime

For in this stillness all we can hear

Is our breath like ocean waves so clear

Listen well to the ebb and the flow

Where all that resides is the peace we know

And just like the giants of our seas

We travel through space so utterly freed.

Epic

You were born an epic success story
But maybe you forgot or couldn't see
Yet the timeless mind and heart of it all
Will patiently remind you to recall.

Let me listen

'I'm just sayin' that while you're there
And need something to soothe your cares
Speak up, speak up, speak up so clear
To the sky where words disappear

Let the breeze take them even higher
As if they're ashes from a fire
Speak up, speak up, speak up so clear
Until no more words can appear

When you're done take a minute or two
To hear the message just for you
Only listen, no need or trying
What's left when no words are flying?

Can you hear the beat in your heart
That one place where nothing's apart?
A peaceful silence kind of thing
And a calming joy it does bring.

The door of possibility

If no one ever told you this
That this door can even exist
Then maybe you feel held back
By feelings of helplessness and lack

But this poem speaks a knowing
And a truth that it is showing
As this door reigns open wide
Bringing better options with its tide

You may not know exactly how
But keep it open and allow
For better possibilities
To fill you up like abundant seas.

Woman empowered

I saw my flaws exposed and raw
My heavy heart strewn on the floor
I could not see how to revive
Ignite my spark or come alive

There I lay in my mirrored wall
Facing this inevitable fall
Funny thing is that in this hour
All my critics had no power

And as I lay next to my heart
Not knowing then how to start
I'd see my heart beat on and on
Showing me just how to be strong

My heart in this vulnerable state
Was the epitome of great
As her persistence guided me
Back to innocence where I am free.

This heroine

This heroine, at the centre of it all
Is indeed me, myself that I must recall
And from a place of love, a script I now write
Holding my heroine in the brightest light

I must then take care with every page
Consult my intuition and inner sage
Be patient and gentle as the words come through
Always writing what's in my heart and what's true

Checking in and asking is this really her?
Is it her choice and is it what she prefers?
Keeping in mind her core values and mission
Giving her courage and granting permission

Bringing in characters that support her dreams
Plenty of resources bursting at the seams
Opportunities and concepts flowing free
Focus, determination and clarity

This heroine is my greatest creation
As her thoughts and actions can bring such elation
I'll be sure to take care and write a story
That allows her to shine in all her glory!

The fragrance of self-love

The lavender oil in my hot shower

The vibrant smell of roses in flower

The fresh mown grass on those bright summer days

The waft of clean linen sheets as I laze

The whiff of earthy potatoes roasting

The aroma of sourdough bread toasting

The zingy hit of lemon and ginger

The warm delight of coffee that lingers

The joy of coconut on sun kissed skin

The sense of relaxation from within

The aura of good vibes that infiltrate

And the olfactory of this higher state.

Nurture the senses

Sweetest soul, you're a beautiful flower
Desiring to come into your power
But bees only come when you open right up
Thus expanding and fulfilling your cup

Think of your senses as petals therefore
Nurturing them well to their very core
Stimulate each one with such great pleasure
For herein lies the hidden gold treasure.

Trust the process

Breaking open hearts my love
Was always going to take some pain
For letting go of feeling small
Will make you become whole again

Unconditional love requires
No one standing in ivory towers
So, shining your purest light right now
May dazzle some souls who fear to allow

Please trust the process keep it going
The more you expand you'll carry on flowing
The flower of life will bloom for all
And collectively you hear its call.

I'll not be hung by my own tongue

I'll not be hung

By my own tongue

These words I speak

Are the peace I seek

Hate will contract

Bringing more lack

I must then see

Love sets me free

One love can reign

For peace again.

Best dream

I am embodying my best dream
Into my live reality stream
This dream is driven by my heart's field
Where endless possibilities yield
Even if my head questions it all
I trust and into my heart free fall.

Dreams are born

And into the silence I go

Beyond everything I know

The realm where love and peace does reign

For in here, I feel whole again

I float a while in this domain

Where feelings never need a name

An effortless flow I can bring

Into every note that I sing

This greater power was always mine

It resides beyond space and time

The grandest Creation of all

Is asking me to hear its call

The more I bring forth this peace

The more confusion will thus cease

And greater still my dreams will bloom

Because they are born from this womb.

Heart

My heart's not afraid
It's of ancient stardust made
Where true peace lies laid.

Peaceful space is fertile earth

Peace is the truest power

No victim here need cower

No bully with loyal crowds

No endless self imposed shrouds

Peace is like a canvas blank

All that has passed we can thank

Forgive it too - let it go

To start a new and better show

Claiming peace is brave indeed

By whichever faith or creed

Peaceful space is fertile earth

Where reigns all that we are worth.

I know

This well of everything contains it all

Into its vastness I let myself fall

Then when I rise, I rise on each wing

That knows exactly what makes my heart sing

I know of kindness and gentle touch

I know of compassion and loving so much

I know that change can bring the new

I know all feelings can pass on through

I know that my focus is the key

I know like a lens I am the clarity

I know it only takes this knowing

For all of this to keep on growing.

My song

I've a resonance and it's all my own
But alas I let it be overthrown
I lost it in all the debris and mess
Yet now this truth is okay to confess

I have danced too long to tunes I don't know
Have left my joints in ways I cannot grow
Barely able to recognise myself
For my own true song was left on the shelf

Now I rise up to reclaim my true song
I'm listening well and listening long
It may take a while but it's coming back
I am realigning with my own tracks

It even feels strange to return to me
When for so long I did not feel this free
But my song will keep playing on and on
Waiting for me to be my true person.

DUCKING AWESOME

Of course, I'm ducking awesome through and through
And yes, YOU there reading this are awesome too
That thing, that essence that brings us the bees
The majestic and even tiny trees
Oceans, currents and life in flow
All the delicious food we grow
The rainbows, showers, warming sun
Everything since time had begun
This thing that brought you into being
Giving you eyes for all you're seeing
Smells and touch, and amazing sound
The air, the atoms and solid ground
Is all of you and yes, all of me
You're so ducking awesome, do you see?

If life

If life is creation
And you're the creator
Then take plenty of time
To create the sublime.

A wealth of what's true

It's crazy, I forgot I'm at the helm
Got swept away by storms and overwhelmed
But heck, it's MY movie this time around
And I am the symphony making sound

It's time for this heroine to show up
And write a juicy script from her full cup
Enough pain and emotion has passed through
To give this story a wealth of what's true.

Who is pulling the strings?

See these strings of vibrant light
That in free motion so delight
But hindered by fearful illusion
Cause chaos and utter confusion

These strings were made to play so free
Like an instrument in harmony
But harmonies cannot be played
When they're out of tune and afraid

I'd love to say the time is now
Such harmonies we do allow
We must remember the light is on
Here now, in every single person

Strings of light all over the place
Like Christmas sparkle in every space
Can we stop and ask one thing
Who is pulling our own light strings?

Great intelligence

The same energy that breathes

That fills our lungs and the trees

Is everywhere and in sync

And it doesn't miss a blink

Such great intelligence reigns

It talks to us through our pains

Tells us to open our minds

Where vast treasures we can find

From the quiet we are shown

To let go of all we've known

And not think we must know how

But be trusting and allow

Feeling in our hearts what's right

No need for weapons and fight

We know what's good and what's kind

A boundary enough we'll find

So, with love and open minds

Collectively we'll then find

That with no effort or strain

We can live in peace again.

The true essence of your being

It doesn't matter what comes and goes
Thoughts and feelings, and all one's woes
Because they are simply passing through
They are not your presence and what is true

So observe a while these fantastic creatures
Witness their outline and all their features
Take comfort in knowing they are only temporary
Illusions if you like, not real or scary

Absolutely nothing can compare
Or even allow you to prepare
For knowing the true essence of your being
But when you do, it is so wonderfully freeing.

Nope, not a ping pong ball…

I am not a ping pong ball
At the mercy of it all
Nor the crazy outside world
Where reactions are unfurled

I'm awake and I'm aware
To contemplate and to care
To not react like I'm done
But to behave like I've won!

Empowered

Empowered am I who takes some time
To sit and watch all feelings of mine
Without judgement or needing to solve
I trust this process as I evolve

Letting my need to react pass through
Helps me see the bigger picture view
From this plane of observing with care
My sight is clearer and less impaired

So too I listen to all of me
My body, my thoughts and all I 'see'
I then learn about myself much more
Allowing my intelligence to pour

When I'm not held back by my feelings
I break through all limiting ceilings
I am free to make better choices
To learn and listen to wise voices.

'When...'

When you're done searching, I am here.

And I'm loving you.

When you've stopped proving any point. I am here.

And I'm loving you.

When you're on your knees and given up. I am here.

And I'm loving you.

When you're soaring high with success. I am here.

And I'm loving you.

When you're pained and tense. I am here.

And I'm loving you.

When you feel humiliated and belittled, I am here.

And I'm loving you.

When you smile and breathe deep. I am here.

And I'm loving you.

Always and forever I am here. I never left.

No need to rush or race

If you lay every brick of your house with care and grace

You'll see there's absolutely no need to rush or race.

But here I am and here I'll stay

Never is the sharp wind too cold

Nor the dimly lit sky too dark

To keep you from my gentle state

I'm always here beyond those gates

The wind, the moods and dimness too

Plus all kinds of other feelings

Will always pass and make their way

But here I am and here I'll stay.

The whole world needs a brand new game

No set amount of time can heal
Deep wounds we've tried to conceal

Pain from many a generation
Takes much love for regeneration

Only now we set the pain free
By giving it space to just be

No more fighting or passing blame
The whole world needs a brand new game.

Einstein said it well and clear

Something could well be squeezing you
And it's for very good reason
It is questioning you right now
Because love, it is the season

The absolute time to wake up
To access your own great power
Alter and change your inner state
Blossom just like a spring flower

Leave all the past and woes behind
Focus only on the present
Because only in the right now
You can accept what you've been sent

This mighty gift has come your way
As Einstein said it well and clear
That it's your imagination
Which helps overcome any fear

It's not what we were all once taught
So, we remember yet again
It may just take a little while
But efforts will not be in vain.

What do you so treasure?

What do you so treasure
That has no sure measure
But makes you smile so wide
And lets all woes subside?

What do you so treasure
Take great lengths in pleasure
Dream of in darker climes
Sing loud in brighter times?

What do you so treasure
That you seek at leisure
And take much comfort in
Bringing more peace within?

Could it be that treasures
Need no special measures
Or any strain and strife
Just refocusing life?

Could it be that treasures
And all of life's pleasures
Are always in our view
Where we let love shine through?

The future

Wow, how liberating it is to me
That the future we so wish to see
Is made by every choice we make
So, let's pause before each step we take

Will each choice bring better balance
Nurture children and their talents
With what we decide, will it nurture earth
Invest in future generations worth?

The seeds we plant in physical form
Will they benefit all babies born?
Somehow every choice Is easier now
Driven by the future we wish to allow.

Away from the noise

Away from the noise
We can better poise
Find stillness of mind
Be better aligned.

Like an eagle

I am the captain of my own ship
And if I'm not sufficiently equipped
For all the storms that are rising high
I'll settle here instead for a while

In a warm place of shelter and peace
I gather myself into one piece
Breathing deep and into dreams I go
Where only peace and harmony grows

In my dreams the thermal gives me height
Like an eagle I have perfect sight
Soaring above the lakes and the sea
And the storms are nowhere near to me.

Listening to silence will break the chains

The silence will tell us who we are
How we are loved and have come so far
It'll tell us we can start again
Move onwards from past hurt and pain

And even if the confusion reigns
Listening to silence will break the chains
Because all best stories start from here
Where love and peace are so very clear

 Waking up can cause confusion
From all the structural illusion
Questioning beliefs and all the facts
Looking for answers in old tracks

But renewal begins in the now
In the present, the truth we allow
The silence will tell us all is well
And the stories we prefer to tell.

Hammock

I cannot quite believe my luck
I'm cradled inside this hammock
In a place that's ethereal
I'm the most fluid I could feel

Somewhere in the distance are whales
And ships on soft breeze that do sail
But I'm all settled on this land
Swinging gently above the sand.

The Donut poem

Nothing to be fixed here
This wholeness is all clear
My donut spins in peace
Love do-nut ever cease.

Everyone is born from the womb

Everyone's born from the womb

Yet this womb is not a tomb

Not a dark, forgotten room

But the place where love resumes

We must nurture its sweet tune

And encourage it to bloom.

Beaten path

Those who seek magic will find it some way
When off the beaten path they will have strayed.

Earth's soil

The earth's soil I feed
With the love I need
Does make my roots thrive
And joy come alive.

For the beauty of less pressure

With all the rush of pressure and such
And when overwhelm is just too much
The slower our pace the greater the ease
Giving way for all tension to cease
When water flows in slower motion
The more we feel peaceful emotion
For the sun dances more gently then
Onto water that's calmer again.

Higher road

I intend to take the higher road
It relieves me of a heavy load
Accepting the things I cannot change
Helping my consciousness be rearranged

Letting be all their judgements and scorn
These traits were never meant to be worn
This higher road is much less bleak
And herein lies the peace I seek.

For the wonder of it

I wonder with wondering eyes

How this world looks with brighter skies

I wonder when people will smile

When their worries are gone a long while

I wonder when we'll feel relieved

Heard and respectfully perceived

And waves of kindness permeate

Every mindset and every state

I wonder when I'll walk through towns

See all souls with their rightful crowns

Going about their day with grace

With no masks to burden each face.

Perhaps

Perhaps the greatest strength and most noble feat
Is to love yourself when you feel incomplete.

Take your time

Take your time my sweet
Rest deep in your seat
Feel what you must feel
Let love be the seal

Feel your breath as flow
Fluid it does know
Soothing everything
Such peace it can bring.

Baked peaches

Baked peaches and cream on warm summer days
Stuffing my face like it's the latest craze
Then running barefoot on velvety grass
Hoping for this moment to always last

Rocking to and fro on a swing in trees
Blissful and heavenly are days like these
When the sun does dip and hangs low above
I'll be singing songs of this joy I loved.

Peace I know

If by my breath I am alive
And have such potential to thrive
Then, by my breath the gold will flow
For my dreams to flourish and grow

So, I will breathe in love so deep
My body its wealth I will keep
Then, as I gently let it go
I return to the peace I know.

The best exchange rate

I've been given this gift of today
My gratitude I wish to repay
But I wonder then what I can do
To express my thanks all this day through

Perhaps just a warm smile I can bring
And an uplifting song I can sing
Will suffice enough for me to know
That on repeat this feeling will grow

I wonder too if I'll be ignited
To do some things that make me excited
Or just wallow in a peaceful state
Either way, it's the best exchange rate!

Forest glade

The magic of this forest glade
Feels calming and divinely made
The light streams through in stripes and strings
Moving gently as if it sings

The path that snakes gently through it
Is soothing and heavenly lit
In the distance the barn owl calls
And the flow of the water falls

All around are shadows dancing
Of deer amongst the trees prancing
Birds and squirrels dart here and there
In harmony in this home they share.

Cocooned

I have blanket upon blanket ruched up on my lap
The sun is shining warmth through the window on tap
So bright are the rays I have to squint my eyes
But this golden light is a most uplifting prize

I feel cocooned in love like endless cashmere
I'm teary with joy and let loose a free tear
I'm so at deep peace with this moment in time
Plus I know I can return for this moment is mine.

Pink sun

The enormous and pink setting sun
With edges soft that start to run
Spilling onto the horizon now
And even onto waves somehow

The warmth and glow spreads really wide
Across the slow incoming tide
The clear water meets my toes to tease
But I barely move, I'm too at ease

Gently it rises up my feet
Washing over them, so discreet
The saltiness makes my toes tingle
While they squelch through sand and mingle

I may just stay here for a while
Even walk for another mile
Letting the sun kiss my soft face
All worries here leave without trace.

Free

I am free and have been freed

When I've no need to succeed

I have no expectations

I'm without limitations

All my fears fall apart

When I follow my heart

All stress does then cease

When I'm rooted in peace

With nothing to juggle

I'm without any struggle

And with nothing to gain

I am without the pain.

Thrive to the max

That force which created my life
Is far greater than any strife
It pours through me with every breath
It lives long past every death

It's the essence of all we know
The truth of abundant flow
It beats and reigns in my chest
And so ends every conquest

So vast and mysterious too
Yet through my eyes it shines through
With this flow of such power
I'm reminded never to cower

As I shift my consciousness here
To the truth that makes all clear
I can see that I can relax
And thrive to the very max.

Ready

Suspended in space where all is well

Ready for this great story to tell

A story of plenty that is everywhere

Love pouring freely for all to share

Time here is timeless and always enough

Making more room for resting and stuff

Abundance is plentiful and on tap

There are no limits or sealing cap

Ideas flow forth in majestic fashion

As do the fires of your heart's passion

But so does your vision and dreams come true

Effortlessly streaming through your world and you.

Cast in stone

You are many things my love
But you are not cast in stone
So like a flowing river
Dance like you've never known.

The Kindness diet

I'm feeding myself on the kindness diet
I'm over here preparing and quiet
I've needed time away to realise
How much I can create with kinder eyes

In the quiet at first, I heard the critics tongue
But her thoughts and feelings left me burnt and stung
I knew I had to feed on thoughts more kind
So, here in my heart, the kindness I did find.

The dream I always knew somehow

How fast we run toward our dreams
Yet right here, a harmony streams
Breathing it in through every part
In this present, where dreams do start

Right up through our toes and feet
Up to our head where bliss does meet
Breathing in this harmony now
Is the dream I always knew somehow.

The door of possibility

If no one ever told you this
That this door can even exist
Then maybe you feel held back
By feelings of helplessness and lack

But this poem speaks a knowing
And a truth that it is showing
As this door reigns open wide
Bringing better options with its tide

You may not know exactly how
But keep it open and allow
For better possibilities
To fill you up like abundant seas.

I am the Garden of Eden

I am the Garden of Eden
I reside within and without
So, tend to me and keep me real
By sowing your love all about

Use your imagination then
To create your garden of bliss
With whatever you prefer indeed
For nothing needs to be amiss

If there are pastures left alone
Or lands abandoned deep within
Then, tend to them by loving them
And let your dear heart always win

This power you have to reform
To recreate all and renew
Will transform any dark corners
And turn muddy waters blue

It's also a power that flows
With the power of other souls
Coming together right now
To harmonize as one true goal.

Basking

I see fairy lights hung from trees
Swinging gently in light breeze
I hear the laughter in the air
Cuz no one here has any care

Basking in this special place
Where nothing needs to be faced
I feel the joy of child-like play
And warmth that longs to always stay

The waves that lap at the shore
Remind me there is always more
And all I need to do right now
Is focus on this and allow

I smell the cedar wood and pine
Knowing this moment is all mine
Walking barefoot and feeling light
All is so well and all is right

My body moves so fluidly
As here it knows it is so free
A harmony I'm listening to
Cuz all my dreams have now come true.

Take a chance

Oh my love, take a chance

On this life's rhythm dance

It may not go exactly right

Your dreams may seem out of sight

But take a chance because you can

Remember how it all began

There's always room for miracles

Life's great and grandest pinnacles

And when the sun's set in warm skies

You'll see that the 'chance' was the prize.

PILLAR OF LIGHT

I see the truth of my inner state
Something that no one can subjugate
I am freedom, love, immensely vast
Much more than all the shadows downcast

I am the pillar of strength and light
The vision and all inner sight
And this remembering is a true gift
Necessary to bring about this shift

Change is imminent and in full force
Driven by the one true source
All is being revealed right now
And the light of heaven is what I allow.

NOT BROKEN

We're not broken you and I
But we've been moulded, shaped and carved
By an out of date system
That has left us feeling starved

That's ok because there's another way
But first we must see that it is true
That this other way is possible
A way that serves us and is completely new

So let's come out of hiding
Come out from behind our tree
There is nothing to be ashamed of
We're bright, beautiful and free

Just one small step at a time
Expressing and hearing our voices
Seeing that we are worthy
Remembering that we have choices

Then as we sink our roots into the ground
Filling the earth with our amazing being
We create a new world that serves us all
A world that is blissful and totally freeing.

A tale with roots...

Of this I am most certainly sure
Where there's water there's always more
The flow of life and all good things
Is through your heart where it sings

Fear not illusory lack and rejection
Focus instead on nature's perfection
With an open heart you can hear it sing
And into life good fortune it'll bring

When you listen to this river dance
That sends you into a kind of trance
You'll be rewarded with such prosperities
A tale rooted in universal verities.

The tiny things

I would writhe and I would squirm
Not wanting to see or to learn
But I didn't know when, what or how
That great abundance, I could allow

The ease came in the tiny things
Because it's in the focus that brings
No matter how small the focus is
The focus itself is the bliss

A raindrop on the leaf of a pine
Reflecting skies transcending time
The smell of rose on summer days
When we'd recline and happily laze

Any kind thought held long enough
Is the focus of loving stuff
Right now in this moment alone
We can make the tiny things know

Sensuality for the the living

Nothing is coerced

When love is put first

Gentle is the touch

That adores so much

All moments bar none

True love's always won

For what we feel now

Next up we allow

Nothing foreboding

Senses exploding

Taste buds ignited

Our hearts excited

Uplifting our souls

With senses of gold

Bring richness to all

And dreams to free fall.

Looking through a different lens

Looking through the most loving lens

Was the signal I had to send

I'm the transmitter of my dreams

And love is bursting from the seams

This universe - the one true song

Knows I am loved and nothing's wrong

The universe loves me and smiles

Giving me nudges all the while.

Rise into peace and our heaven above

A weed is no less worthy of the air it breathes

Than a majestic rose in all its glory

Each playing essential roles

In this fantastic and beautiful story

Feelings are no different to these wonderful plants

Every one of them asking for acceptance and love

And once we have accepted them ALL we are free

To rise into peace and our heaven above.

My heart as head of state

I have become aware
That I cannot compare
My journey is all my own
As I travel back home

I am the love I feel
In a fluid motion reel
Vibrating at such a rate
With my heart as head of state.

You are the stuff that galaxies are made

There may or may not always be a critic
Trying to sabotage or be even more horrific
But hear me now and hear me well
This is the truth I am about to tell

There is no place anymore to be afraid
You are the stuff that galaxies are made
And within you, throughout and all around
Is the most magnificent and beautiful sound

The sound of love, support and eternal flow
Always here in the audience of your show
So never doubt and never stop expressing
And together we'll be forever coalescing.

thANKH you

Into love we fall

By thanking it all

Unlocking the door

That bound us before

We've opened our hearts

And ready to start

With no more lock down

We can see all around

With a lens that's clear

We can better steer

And travel as ONE

By knowing love's won.

I wonder

I wonder if I start this day

With joy in my heart and let it stay

I wonder if I let all burdens pass

Release all stress and tension fast

I wonder if I allow love to reign

To feel deep comfort again and again

I wonder if I can also feel wealthy

Not least, super fit and utterly healthy

I love to wonder for wondering sake

For these feelings are real, not fake

Wondering free and playing this way

Help my best dreams come my way.

A wide, open heart attracts all the gold

Here's a story you may not have been told
A wide, open heart attracts all the gold
In times gone past things didn't last
The lie of lack was the message cast

But the barrier encasing a tender heart
Only strengthens the illusion we're apart
So remove the cage and let us unite
Because as ONE there is no need to fight

And as WE ARE ONE all is ours
No one sitting in ivory towers
There's so much abundance for ONE and all
We only have to listen to this call.

We, the unconquered soul incarnate

The deepest, darkest depth of the sea

Is also vibrating effortlessly

And from this depth a tune of love

Can lift and resonate higher above

No matter what pain we have endured

We can remember that it has been cured

In the fluid movement of our being

Our song and dance is what is freeing

We, the unconquered soul incarnate

Have come here to remember our true fate

That our world is not set or cast in stone

But is a glorious song of which we CHOOSE the tone.

I'm actually really lucky

I'm actually really lucky that I can read and write

That I have Hearing, Smell, Taste, Touch and Sight

That I have the means to create unique art

Which reflects this world of which I am a part

To be able to see the beauty around me

And express it how I wish is so flippin' easy

I'm actually lucky to be impatient like a child

Knowing that my excitement is alive and wild

That also I have learned to slow down a bit

So that I can observe more while in transit

And also to have experienced some suffering

Because into this world compassion I can bring

I'm actually really lucky for all of it, you see

As it goes full circle and all comes back to me.

Acknowledgements

There are too many people and things I want to thank that'll fit onto this page. However, in brief, thank you to my husband, all my family, pets, friends, customers, acquaintances and more. I do want to thank some people who have specifically helped **steer** me onto a brighter path through their work. In no particular order:

Author Ester Hicks - *'It Is Not about Controlling Thoughts, It Is about Guiding Thoughts.'* *'Stop arguing for your limitations.'* *'Power is joy, power is love, power is appreciation, power is clarity, power is knowing, power is the universe flowing through your fingertips!'*

Author Jaclyn Johnston - *'The point is fear will always be dancing around in your mind, but how you choose to respond to it is where manifestations take place. You manifest based upon your focus.'*

Dr Joe Dispenza - *'The biggest lie we've been told is that we're linear beings living a linear life. We are dimensional beings, living dimensional lives.'*

Author, speaker and poet G Brian Benson -

'A Minute of Failure

A minute of failure can lead one to grow
Or tumble and stumble to the depths far below
The decision is yours, what to do when you fall
To pack up and quit or stand firm and tall

Everyone fails, it's natural and true
It's part of the process to grow and become new
So pick yourself up and give try again
If you find yourself failing, it's a fleeting trend

Don't give in to failure or you will never be set free
It's for those who don't believe, and lack vision to truly see
Keep standing, keep standing, each time you fall down
Your true nature will emerge, your spirit unbound.'

Copyright 2008 G. Brian Benson.

Space for your notes, poems or doodles…

Space for your notes, poems or doodles…

Space for your notes, poems or doodles…

Space for your notes, poems or doodles…